A PORTFOLIO OF

HOME
OFFICE
IDEAS

COWLES
Creative Publishing

CONTENTS

© Copyright 1998
Cowles Creative Publishing, Inc.
5900 Green Oak Drive
Minnetonka, Minnesota 55343
1-800-328-3895
All rights reserved

Printed in U.S.A.
Library of Congress
Cataloging-in-Publication Data
A portfolio of home office ideas.
        p. cm.
    ISBN 0-86573-889-0 (softcover)
    1. Home offices. 2. Interior decoration. I. Cowles Creative
Publishing.
NK2195.O4P67 1998
747.7'9--dc21   98-7294

Associate Creative Director: Tim Himsel
Editorial Director: Bryan Trandem
Managing Editor: Jennifer Caliandro
Project Manager: Michelle Skudlarek
Writer: Anne Price Gordon
Editor: Karl Larson
Art Directors: Kathleen Bruzelius, Kari Johnston
Copy Editor: Janice Cauley
Vice President of Development
    Planning & Production: Jim Bindas
Production Manager: Patt Sizer

Printed on American paper by R. R. Donnelley & Sons Co.

COWLES
Creative Publishing, Inc.
Minnetonka, Minnesota, USA
President: Iain Macfarlane
Group Director, Book Development: Zoe Graul
Creative Director: Lisa Rosenthal
Senior Managing Editor: Elaine Perry

Other Portfolio of Ideas books include:

A Portfolio of Kitchen Ideas
A Portfolio of Deck Ideas
A Portfolio of Landscape Ideas
A Portfolio of Bathroom Ideas
A Portfolio of Window & Window Treatment Ideas
A Portfolio of Flooring Ideas
A Portfolio of Bedroom Ideas
A Portfolio of Unique Deck Ideas
A Portfolio of Lighting Ideas
A Portfolio of Water Garden & Specialty Landscape Ideas
A Portfolio of Porch & Patio Ideas
A Portfolio of Storage Ideas
A Portfolio of Fireplace Ideas
A Portfolio of Ceramic & Natural Tile Ideas
A Portfolio of Fence & Gate Ideas
A Portfolio of Outdoor Furnishing Ideas
A Portfolio of Home Spa Ideas

Photos on page two (top to bottom) courtesy of Turnstone/
Steelcase, Inc., Sauder Woodworking Co., and Levenger.
Photos on page three (top to bottom) courtesy of Levenger,
Vitra, Inc., and Levenger.

Photos on cover (clockwise) courtesy of Reliable HomeOffice,
Vitra, Inc., Reliable HomeOffice, Room & Board, and Levenger.

Natural light helps to create *a comfortable work environment. The large window permits ample sunlight and, with the light-colored paint on the walls, creates a comfortable work environment.*

WHAT MAKES A GREAT HOME OFFICE?

Not many years ago, the thought of working from home was considered a fantastic vision of the distant future. However, with more and more people setting up home offices every day, it is clear that future has arrived earlier than many expected.

You may be interested in a home office because you are starting your own business, telecommuting or in need of a space to tend to household paperwork such as paying bills, doing taxes or keeping tabs on investments.

Depending on your needs, a great office may be a pull-down desk in the kitchen or a fully furnished setup in the basement. Still, no matter what type of home office you want to create, the goal is the same: a home office should have a comfortable, logical design that makes it easy to do the business at hand.

In essence, a home office is a fairly simple concept, but arranging one requires some careful consideration and planning. You will need to select a location, choose lighting and purchase office furniture and desk accessories. Without a game plan, you may end up with a home office that is inefficient and impractical, and more expensive than you had planned.

This book helps you develop a strategy for planning and creating your own home office. The Planning section provides useful insight into selecting a location and arrangement. The section entitled Essentials is a guide to many of the products and decorating ideas for home offices. Armed with this information, you can review the Portfolio section to learn how these elements can be brought together in different ways to create a home office that is right for you.

Photo courtesy of Reliable HomeOffice

A space directly above a stairway can easily accommodate a simple office setup. The glass block wall brings in natural sunlight and offers privacy that cannot be had with conventional windows. Glass block is also used for a short partition wall at the back of the office.

(left) **A converted armoire** has room for a computer and printer, as well as shelf space for often-referenced materials. When not in use, the armoire doors can be closed to conceal the office equipment.

(opposite) **A bedroom office** can make use of existing furniture, such as a dresser and small desk. A bedroom office can be ideal for students.

(below) **This office with an L-shaped desk** has plenty of worksurface area. The Persian rug gives the room color and serves as a mat for the roller chair. The file and drawer cabinet is set on wheels so it can be easily moved around.

Planning
IDENTIFYING YOUR NEEDS

A home office can take many forms, some of them quite simple. What is sometimes called the "kid's workstation" often includes a child-sized desk and chair, a computer and a drawer or two. For general family use, having a large desktop may be more important than setting up elaborate storage and filing systems. But if you're planning to start a full-fledged business that requires frequent client meetings, you'll need a full array of office equipment, and you'll need to set aside space for a conference table and perhaps even a reception area.

Before you begin to spend hundreds or thousands of dollars on a home office, it's well worth taking some time to think about what its primary use will be. Do you need a space to connect with the outside world via fax, computer modem and telephone? Do you want a place that is removed from the rest of the house so you can work on a presentation in peace? Or would you simply like a comfortable spot for you and the kids to surf the Internet, play a few computer games or work on an occasional project? In short, why do you want a home office? Answering this question is the single most important step of the planning process since it's the only way you'll be sure to end up with the right home office.

Once you've identified how your home office will be used, it's time to make a key list of necessities, including the furniture, equipment, accessories, electrical service and telephone lines required for the work you plan to do. Certain kinds of work require specialized tools or setups; for example, graphic designers or architects often need drawing tables and oversized lateral shelves to hold their work. Putting together a list of must-have items will help you move forward with the planning process, since it will directly affect your decisions regarding the location and layout of your home office.

Photo courtesy of Broyhill Furniture Industries, Inc.

*A **compact home office** can be situated in an underused corner so as not to impose on other areas of the house. In this example, an unobtrusive office is tucked behind a large growing plant that creates a privacy partition.*

(right) **A portable book stand** *allows you to read and do paperwork from a comfortable armchair. A pivoting worksurface adjusts to the most comfortable angle, and a horizontal surface holds beverages or snacks. A portable book stand is a helpful accessory for any type of home office.*

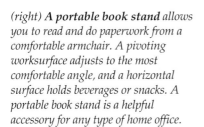

Photo courtesy of Levenger

Photo courtesy of Levenger

Photo courtesy of Andersen Windows, Inc.

A home office should be designed *for its primary user. In this artist's studio, the desk, computer and other standard office appointments have been omitted in favor of an easel, drop cloths and model's daybed. Skylights provide the ample natural light crucial to an artist's work.*

Planning
CHOOSING A LOCATION

As you consider the possible locations of your home office, keep an open mind. A home office can be located almost anywhere you want. In addition to the kitchen, spare bedroom, basement or attic, there are many places that are often overlooked, such as a closet, the space under a stairway or even a large hallway. As you select a location for your home office, keep in mind the following important elements.

Square footage. Unless you plan to build an addition to your house, space for a home office is usually limited. Still, it's helpful to measure and compare different locations. While comparing areas, keep in mind how your list of necessities will fit in each location and be aware that it's easy to underestimate the need for space.

Access. Depending upon your needs, your home office can share a space used for other purposes, or it can be a dedicated space that is separate from the rest of your living space. A family office, for example, might best be located in the living room, where everyone can get at it, while a home-based business with many clients may require even a separate entrance.

Power supply. If you anticipate a need for much office equipment, adequate wiring and outlets (i.e., GFCIs) can be critical. Even if your work doesn't require a computer, chances are you'll need more outlets or phone jacks.

(opposite) *An entry hallway* that sees little use can provide space for a small office. Situated in a nook with shelves lining the opposite wall, this previously unused space has been transformed into a practical office setting.

(right) *A computer workstation* can easily fit into an attic or loft. Such a space is ideal for work that requires concentration and privacy. High temperatures and humidity can be hard on computer equipment, however, so make sure your attic is well ventilated or air-conditioned.

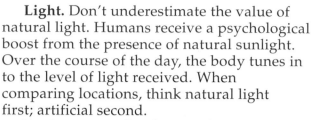

Photo courtesy of Artemide Inc.

Light. Don't underestimate the value of natural light. Humans receive a psychological boost from the presence of natural sunlight. Over the course of the day, the body tunes in to the level of light received. When comparing locations, think natural light first; artificial second.

Environment. Good air quality and a comfortable climate are essential for your well-being and productivity. Ideally, the location you choose should have windows. If you're converting a non-living space, like a garage or attic, take into account any heating, ventilation or air-conditioning needs.

Noise level. Make sure the noise level in your space is acceptable. Though some people love working with the sound of radio and other background noise, other people require complete silence. When choosing a space for your home office, evaluate the noise levels during the period when you'll be working.

Photo courtesy of American Woodmark

(above) ***These light fixtures*** *with stylish shades provide indirect lighting that is more appealing than fluorescent. A dimmer switch can regulate the light to whatever level you desire.*

(left) ***A kitchen hutch*** *may have enough space to take care of simple paperwork, such as paying monthly bills and writing correspondence.*

(opposite) ***Home offices*** *don't always require dedicated spaces. A hideaway bed makes this guest room a dual-purpose space. With the bed folded away, the room becomes a spacious office.*

Photos courtesy of Techline Furniture

Planning
CREATING A FLOOR PLAN

Once you've chosen a location and decided what needs to go in your home office, it's time to lay out a floor plan. This can be the most enjoyable part of planning, since it gives you a chance to experiment with a variety of ideas.

Begin by taking a look at a few of the most popular configurations shown here, then turn the page for more information and tools you can use to create a working plan for your home office.

WALL OR STRIP LAYOUT

File Cabinet 20" × 15"

Desk 24" × 60"

Bookshelf 12" × 24"

Chair 18" × 18"

L-SHAPED LAYOUT

File Cabinet 20" × 15"

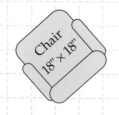

Chair 18" × 18"

Desk 24" × 60"

Table 24" × 60"

Wall or strip layout. This layout is quite simple, with the desk and any bookshelves or storage cabinets lined along one wall. A wall layout may be a good choice if you have limited floor space; however, it's less efficient than other layouts, since the elements aren't always within easy reach.

L-shaped layout. Although this arrangement is natural for a corner, it can also be used to divide the space in the room. You could, for instance, arrange your workstation so the "L" faces out into the room, rather than running it flush against the wall. Either way, the L-shaped layout gives you fairly easy access to a large worksurface.

PARALLEL OR CORRIDOR LAYOUT

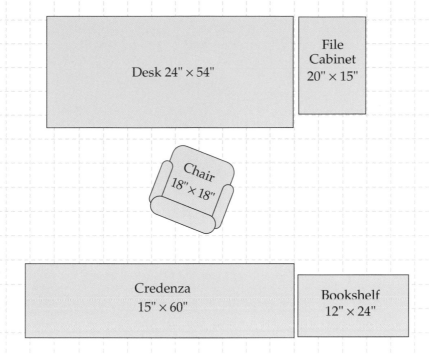

Parallel or corridor layout. In this arrangement, there are two desks or tables set a few feet apart from each other with a chair in between. With a parallel layout, it's easy to separate your work by task; for example, you could set your computer on one surface and put your files and phone on the other.

HORSESHOE OR U-SHAPED LAYOUT

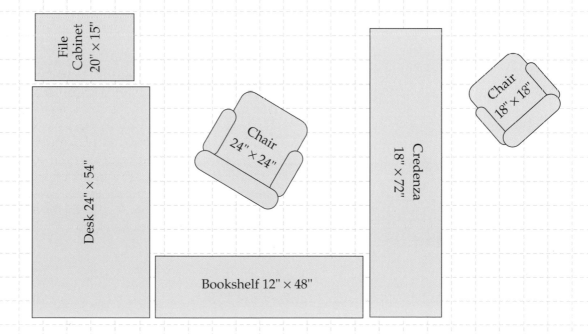

Horseshoe or U-shaped layout. This layout offers perhaps the most efficient use of space, since you have everything you need right within reach. You can even use one end of the "horseshoe" as a mini conference area by adding a chair on the outside edge. Some people, however, felt confined when working in a "U" configuration.

To create a floor plan, make an overall base drawing of the space where you plan to set up your home office. Measure the space, and transfer those measurements to the grid sheet (each square can represent 1 square foot in the room). Measure and add markings to show the location of outlets, windows and any other significant features in the space.

Now go back to your list of office necessities, and make a cutout for large items, such as desks, filing cabinets, chairs and tables, using the templates shown below.

Try out different ideas for your floor plan by arranging and rearranging the cutouts on the base drawing. As you experiment with these and other layout ideas, make sure the arrangements won't block electrical outlets, windows and doorways, and that drawers and doors will open freely.

Once you have a layout that works, you're ready to begin selecting the furniture and equipment to create your new home office.

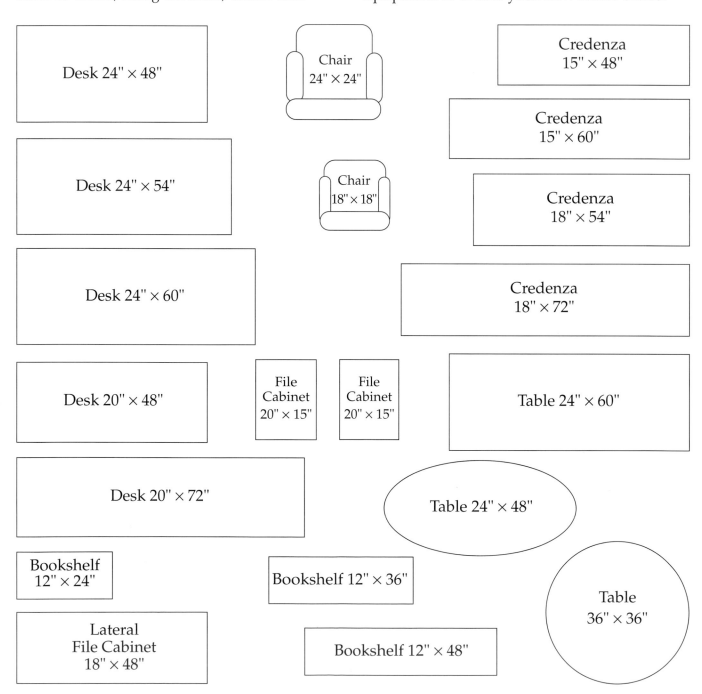

You can use the grid sheet and the sample cutouts provided here to make your floor plan; before starting, make a few photocopies of each page.

Planning
ERGONOMICS

The evolution of the personal computer has brought with it increased interest in ergonomics—the study of how we physically interact with the tools we use. People now realize that the arrangement of a desk, chair, computer screen and keyboard can have adverse effects on health, if these elements cause strain. Carpal tunnel syndrome is just one problem that can arise from an unhealthy setup. Fortunately, an ergonomic work setup doesn't require spending a fortune on specialized equipment; you just need to keep in mind the following basic points.

Measure up. Ergonomists have studied the situation and established a few guidelines that are worth following. The ideal desk height is 28" above the floor; the ideal computer keyboard height is lower, about 23" to 27". Use a wrist pad to bring your wrists up, level with the computer keyboard; this will reduce strain to your hands, arms and shoulders.

Keep an eye out. Computer monitors are often blamed as a cause of eyestrain, but lighting in the work area is often the real culprit. Screen glare can be very hard on your eyes, so avoid placing your monitor opposite a window or other light source that will be reflected off the computer screen. It is also hard on your eyes to work in a high-contrast setting, so try to keep the ambient and task light levels within close range of each other.

Photo courtesy of Ergonomic Logic, Inc.

(*opposite*) **Ergonomic accessories** *can decrease the strain of repetitive work. Some of the accessories available include: a chair with adequate lumbar support, footrests, armrests, an ergonomically correct keyboard and a monitor on an adjustable stand. A glare-reduction screen can be attached to the monitor to reduce eyestrain.*

(*right*) **An ergonomic keyboard** *along with adjustable arm supports can prevent carpal tunnel syndrome. Proper height of these items is also critical.*

(*below*) **Ergonomics shouldn't be overlooked** *even in a home office with limited space. This corner desk lets the user face the computer head-on without turning or twisting the neck. It also features a pull-out drawer for the keyboard and a fully adjustable chair.*

This pull-chain lamp, with its three-step pedestal and large, pyramid-style shade, is a modern interpretation of the art deco style. It is a handsome alternative to more utilitarian lamp styles.

A flexible arm lamp allows you to direct the light precisely where you need it. This type of lamp design is perfect for close, detailed work where good illumination is essential.

A modern brass lamp looks handsome in conservative surroundings, but still has modern advantages. This model has a halogen bulb that is brighter and more energy efficient than incandescents.

HOME OFFICE ESSENTIALS

Once you've chosen a location for your home office and planned its layout, you're ready to begin shopping for the elements that will turn an ordinary space into a productive home office. If you haven't shopped for office furnishings and equipment lately, you'll probably be surprised at the options available. The noisy typewriter, harsh desk lamp, bulky desk and filing cabinet that were standard in offices fifty years ago have now given way to sleek, high-tech electronics and space-age furniture.

On the following pages, you'll find a brief discussion of the different options available when choosing the essential elements of today's home office. Today's office supply manufacturers and retailers welcome the business of individual consumers and offer a wide range of products to match any budget and style preference.

LIGHTING

Good lighting is important in a home office and should be given careful consideration. Basically, two types of lighting are needed: indirect, or overall room lighting, and direct, which is used to light work areas. To achieve each of these, you'll need to mix and match a variety of light sources.

For indirect lighting, natural sunlight is the very best choice, since our eyes adapt to it comfortably. Of course, if the location of your home office doesn't provide many windows,

Halogen track lighting can be directed to provide task lighting, accent lighting for decorative accessories, or can be configured for general room illumination.

A classic incandescent lamp is still a good choice for direct lighting in a traditional-style home office. A lamp with two or more bulbs, or one with a three way switch, allows for greater flexibility.

Modern-style lamps come in many designs. This high-tech lamp has a halogen bulb and features a swivel arm and rotating head that allows the light beam to be precisely directed.

exposure to natural light may be minimal. Popular indirect light sources include track lights, recessed ceiling fixtures and floor lamps. The goal with indirect light is to create an overall balanced level of illumination—a good rule is 2 watts of indirect light for every square foot of space.

Direct lighting is often accomplished using table or desk lamps or by aiming overhead track lights at a worksurface. When placing direct lights, avoid creating unnecessary shadows on your worksurface, since this causes eyestrain— try placing desk lamps off to the left side if you're right-handed and to the right if you're left-handed. Also, make sure the placement of lights won't create glare on your monitor.

For either indirect or direct lighting, there are three types of light bulbs you can use: incandescent, fluorescent and halogen. Incandescents are most familiar and are favored

for the warm, yellowish glow they create. Incandescents are available in a wide range of tones and wattages, with clear and frosted finishes. Although fluorescents are less expensive to operate, some office workers complain that fluorescent lighting is less inviting than incandescent sources. Halogen lights have become popular in recent years for the clean, focused white light they produce and their high energy efficiency. They are, however, somewhat expensive, and there has been growing concern about potential fire hazards they create since they become very hot.

Regardless of which type of light fixtures or bulbs you choose, it can be helpful to create a lighting plan that allows some flexibility once it is installed. Dimmers and directional mountings are examples of little extras that can significantly increase lighting options in your home office.

(below) **Gather a variety of paint samples** when choosing the shade for the walls of your home office. The shade you choose should complement the size and lighting of the room.

(opposite) **Hardwood flooring** is practical and attractive in this modern home office. This floor surface cleans up easy and can handle traffic from assistants and clients.

Essentials
WALL & FLOOR COVERINGS

Although you can use almost any kind of wallcovering in a home office, it's helpful to keep a few points in mind.

First, take into account how much work will be involved in installing and maintaining each kind of wallcovering, whether it's paint, wallpaper, paneling or other materials. Painting the walls, for instance, is a quick task compared to wallpapering or installing paneling. Plus, from a budget standpoint, painting is usually the most economical option.

Another factor to consider is how colors can affect the overall sense of light and space in a room. Darker colors absorb light and can make a room seem smaller. So, if you want to make a large space seem cozier, consider decorating with darker colors. Lighter colors, on the other hand, reflect light and can help to create a more spacious feeling in a room. Lighter colors are probably in order when you have a small space or one without much natural light.

A home office is a great place to experiment with unconventional wallcoverings. Materials such as cork paneling and pegboard offer functionality as well as a degree of uniqueness.

It's also a good idea to think about flooring while selecting wallcovering, since these two elements should complement each other. For example, dark flooring might be offset by light colors on the walls.

Whatever wall covering you finally decide on, it's a good idea to keep it simple. A wallpaper with a patterned design can liven up a room, but strong patterns can go out of style quickly. Furthermore, many people find busy patterns to be distracting in a home office.

Depending upon the size of your home office and the material you choose, floor covering can be a significant expense, so it should be chosen with care. In addition to fitting your budget, the primary concerns to keep in mind are appearance, comfort, durability and ease of maintenance.

What looks good in a room is generally a matter of personal taste, but there are a few design tips to consider when choosing floor coverings. As with wall coverings darker colors make a space seem small, brighter colors enlarge the space. A major advantage of dark-colored floor covering is that it hides dirt. If you think you are going to update your home office at a later date, it's best to choose a neutral color and pattern for floor covering, since it's easier to change the look of other elements in the room.

Comfort is also an important factor to keep in mind when choosing floor covering, especially if your work requires a lot of standing or walking back and forth. Wall-to-wall carpeting will provide the most cushioning and warmth, but it can be expensive and is harder to keep clean than other materials, like vinyl or hardwood floors. The most practical type of carpeting is a low-pile commercial-grade style; most are stain-resistant and can handle the wear and tear of foot traffic and office chair wheels rolling back and forth. Another option is to choose conventional cut-pile carpet and get a protective mat to put under your chair and heavy furniture.

From a practical standpoint, resilient vinyl flooring can't be beat. It is durable, easy to clean and inexpensive compared to carpet or hardwood flooring. There are many styles and colors to choose from, and it's fairly easy to install. It does, however, have a less inviting appearance than other materials, and it still requires some care, since the surface can be scuffed or scratched.

One final consideration that can easily be overlooked is soundproofing. You can go to considerable expense having your home office soundproofed, or you can choose some common-sense materials that will reduce noise levels. If you're trying to create a quiet work environment, you may want to use carpeting rather than hard-surface floor coverings like linoleum or ceramic tile. Soft materials reduce the noise level in a room, while hard materials, such as wood and linoleum, won't dampen noise in the least.

Essentials
WINDOW TREATMENTS

Choosing window treatments for your home office can pose a challenge, since there are so many types available: curtains, blinds, shades, valances and shutters, to name a few. To make the selection process easier, it helps to think about what you want in terms of function and appearance.

Practically speaking, window treatments serve an important role, since they can help control overall light levels. If your office has windows with a southern exposure, blinds or shades that can close and completely block out harsh light may be the best choice. Blinds and shades are also ideal if you have the need for privacy. On the other hand, sheer fabric curtains could be a good choice if you just want to mute the intensity of natural light entering the room. Venetian blinds offer the flexibility to fit both of these situations, since they can be easily adjusted throughout the day as the light levels change.

From a design standpoint, window treatments need to complement the existing decor. Each style of window treatment sets a different tone, and that tone needs to fit in with the style established by the furniture, wall-covering, flooring and decorations. If your office furniture and accessories have a "high-tech" appearance, venetian blinds might be a better choice than curtains. However, those same venetian blinds might be too sterile or clinical in a traditionally furnished room. In addition to the type of window treatment you choose, keep in mind that the color, pattern and even the texture of the material used to make the window treatments should fit in with the overall style of the room.

(opposite) **Blinds** *can be adjusted to temper direct sunlight. Blinds also offer more privacy than draperies. In this office, the blinds are consistent with the designer chairs and the metal desk.*

(right) **Draperies mute light** *entering a room. Here, the soft fabric contrasts with the hard desk, computer and chair.*

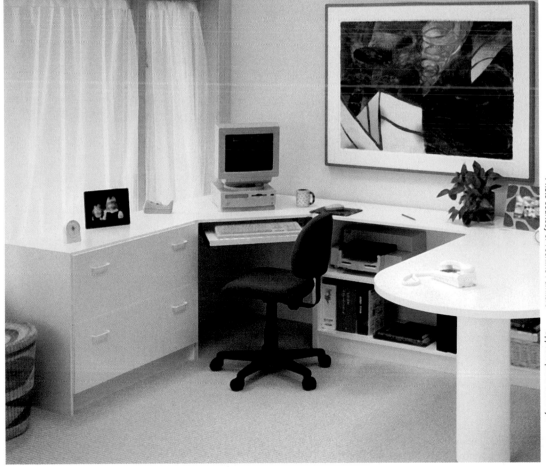

Photo courtesy of Techline Furniture   Opposite photo courtesy of Interlübke

Essentials
DESKS

The centerpiece of any office, large or small, is the desk. Depending upon the location and layout you've chosen for your home office, you may want to use a traditional desk or another type of worksurface altogether. In a kitchen, for example, your "desk" could simply be a section of countertop that you allocate for the office. Regardless of the setting, it helps to think creatively when choosing your primary worksurface.

Space is often the first item to consider when choosing a desk, since it tends to determine your options. If you only have enough space to accommodate a strip layout (see Creating a Floor Plan, pg. 14) and you're on a tight budget, you might want to build your own desk using a long sheet of laminate countertop set on top of a few filing cabinets. Of course, desks come in many other shapes and sizes and are designed to fit a variety of locations and common office-furniture configurations. You'll want to make sure that the desk you choose has an adequate amount of surface area and storage, and that the desk is satisfactory from an ergonomic standpoint (see Ergonomics, pg. 18). This is especially important if you plan to use a computer at your desk; look for desks designed with built-in drawers for the keyboard.

*(opposite) **A semicircular** desk offers plenty of worksurface area without taking up much space. All areas of the desk are easily reached. The arc of the desk contrasts nicely with the checkerboard pattern on the floor. All components roll on casters for easy positioning.*

*(right) **A home office** can easily be integrated into kitchen cabinetry and countertops. One or more drawers and cabinets can be used to store documents and files, while open shelves keep reference materials at easy reach.*

Photo courtesy of KraftMaid Cabinetry, Inc.

Opposite photo courtesy of Reliable HomeOffice

Budget is also an important factor when choosing a desk, particularly since office furniture can be expensive. You may find a bargain by shopping commercial office suppliers who sell used furniture. With the increase in telecommuting and home-based businesses, there are more and more companies that specialize in home office furnishings. These companies offer everything from self-contained "office on wheels" systems, to complete furniture collections. At the top of the line is custom built-in office furniture, which, although costly, can be well worth the investment. With the wide variety of styles and prices available, you're sure to find something that suits your tastes and doesn't demolish your checkbook.

*(left) **The sleek lines** of this designer desk and chair give it an air of sophistication. An independent drawer and file cabinet provides storage.*

*(below) **This oval-shaped desk** has plenty of workspace to keep everything within reach. The cabinets behind the desk are built with wide, flat drawers to store large charts, photographs and sketches.*

Photo courtesy of Roche-Bobois

Photo courtesy of Room & Board

The glass-paneled doors on this armoire cabinet feature wood pulls and a handsome design. Armoire-style office cabinets can hold a surprisingly large number of items, including computer with keyboard, printer and paper, office supplies and reference books. This model also has pop-up side tables mounted on the doors. Closed, the cabinet conceals and protects office equipment, preserving the decor of the room.

(opposite, upper right) **This smaller desk** *has two file drawers and three regular drawers, and is large enough to accommodate a notebook computer.*

(opposite, upper left) **A portable desk** *can be wheeled out of sight when company arrives. The desk has space for the monitor, keyboard and CPU. The laminate surface is durable and comes in a variety of colors.*

(opposite, bottom) **This spacious metal desk** *has a trim design that doesn't detract from the window view. The curved design keeps everything within reach.*

(below) **Consistent styling** *allows this desk to complement the other furniture in this living room. Desk, entertainment center and wall unit all use the same wood and finish. The desk shelves include personal items and decorative accessories that keep with the style of the room.*

DESKS

As you narrow your selection, carefully consider how the desk will look with your decor. You may want to bring in carpet, flooring and wallpaper samples to get an accurate sense of how well the desk will blend with your decorating scheme.

However, it's worth remembering that a home office is a place where you can take a few chances with design. There are no rules, after all. A home office can include traditional furniture used in nontraditional ways. You can create a functional, working desk from a section of countertop, an old dressing table or even a hobby workbench.

Essentials

CHAIRS

Of all the items you will buy for your home office, none is as critical as a good desk chair. Without it, you're destined for backaches and strain to your shoulders, arms and legs, which can result in an overall drop in productivity. A good chair is fully adjustable, so you can set the back, seat and arms exactly where you need them to ensure a "perfect fit." Although these features are usually only found in more expensive chairs, they are worth every penny. You can economize on other seating in your office, but a good desk chair is important.

When shopping for a desk chair, try out your favorite candidates by sitting in each and adjusting all the parts. Look for one that lets you adjust the seat and back in all directions—up and down, back and forth—and also lets you change the tilt position. You should be able to sit comfortably with your feet planted on the floor and your arms relaxed at your sides. Also check to make certain the chair provides adequate lumbar support for your lower back. If you are considering armrests, keep in mind that shorter armrests will allow you to pull the

chair close to the desk. As you look at chairs, it's a good idea to try pulling the chair up to a desk that is the same height as the one you plan to use.

Cushioned chairs can be the most comfortable, but avoid cushioning that is too soft, since it probably won't hold up as well as denser foam materials. Leather is the most durable covering, but you may be satisfied with well-constructed synthetic coverings, too. Many desk chairs are designed with a 5-pronged, star-shaped base on wheels; avoid older designs with only 4 prongs, since these are less stable. Wheels will make it possible to move around quickly. If you have a carpeted floor, you'll need to buy a chair mat.

There are a few other options you may want to consider. A footrest combined with your chair can keep your legs from feeling sluggish. Or take a look at "backless" chairs—they resemble a stool with an angled seat and a bar in front that lets you brace your lower legs against it. These chairs force your spine into an upright, aligned position, and some people find them more comfortable than any other style.

Shorter armrests allow you to pull the chair closer to the desk, which reduces arm strain.

Adequate lumbar support is a fundamental part of any office chair.

Open-weave fabric "breathes" to keep you comfortable.

Adjust the height of the chair for different tasks or users.

The chair sits on a track, so it can slide back and forth.

Five pedestal casters provide stability and easy movement.

The tilt of the chair can be adjusted for a more comfortable angle.

When selecting an office chair, look for a model that blends well with your office's decor and provides the features you need the most. While there will be a variety of chairs available within your budget, consider spending a little more, if necessary, for a chair that looks and feels good.

(far left) **The back and arms** of this chair are made of one piece. This is one of many new designs in office furniture.

(left) **This wood chair** is formed for back and upper leg support. The absence of armrests allows it to be positioned close to any desk. The black lever raises and lowers the seat.

(right) **The stainless steel** arms and the sweeping back that drops down to form the rear legs lend a very modern feel to this pair of chairs. Because their emphasis is on style, they may best serve as seating for clients or visitors.

(below) **The size of these chairs** makes them perfect for smaller rooms. The swivel chair has a gas lift for added comfort. To save space, the side chairs can be stacked.

Essentials
FILING/ORGANIZATION & STORAGE SYSTEMS

Keeping a home office organized is a challenge, especially since there always seems to be something better to do than filing, invoicing or any other administrative task. Even with the best intentions, it's all too easy to start out with a few filing cabinets and shelves that quickly fill up, leaving your desktop and floor overflowing with unfiled paperwork. The only way to avoid this situation is to take the time to review your working style and identify what you need to support it.

It can be helpful to create a flow chart or a simple list of all the steps involved in completing a typical job or project. Though it might seem obvious, you may be surprised to discover how many steps there are and how many of them generate paperwork or require follow-up. Mapping out your work patterns should help you put together a realistic list of what you need to get organized. If you know

that your work generates a lot of paperwork, you'll want to make sure to plan for adequate storage space for filing it. Regardless of the type of work you do, the basic organization and storage elements found in almost any home office setup are filing cabinets, shelving and drawers.

Filing cabinets. In addition to standard vertical and lateral hanging file cabinets, there are many smaller filing units available, some with wheels. Commercial offices are often furnished with open-front filing cabinets; on these, the front lifts up and slides into the unit so you can easily see the contents of the drawer. Also, depending upon the kind of work you do, you may want to look at specialty filing systems, like flat files, which are used to store oversized papers or drawings. Whichever style you choose, look for filing cabinets with well-crafted drawer mechanisms that operate smoothly.

(opposite) **This office hutch** *has a wide desk drawer, two file drawers and a series of open shelves directly above the desk. The cabinets also contain shelving for less frequently used materials.*

(right) **Filing cabinets that match** *the desk in this office create a sense of unity while providing ample storage.*

Shelving. Almost anything goes when it comes to creating or purchasing shelving. You can choose the simplest, no-frills approach by stacking pieces of lumber between concrete or glass blocks, or spend a little more for a basic wall-mounted bracketed shelving system. Freestanding bookcases run the gamut from industrial-strength utility shelves to hardwood designs. And if budget is not an issue, custom built-in bookcases are the best way to provide stylish storage.

Drawers. Though often overlooked, drawer units provide the best storage for many office items. A small drawer cart on wheels, for instance, can be helpful because it is portable. There are also many different types of smaller drawer units that are designed to sit on the desktop. Desktop baskets may be a good choice if you need to review items over and over again as you work.

Office products have come a long way in terms of style, so there's no reason to be confined to dull gray metal filing cabinets or bland shelving. Whatever system you choose, be sure to keep your personal and business documents separate, to avoid confusion and to make it easier to gather information when you file your tax returns.

(above) **These shelves are both stylish** and practical: the wood and simple design complement the other furnishings, while wheels allow the unit to be easily moved.

(right) **Small flat file cabinets** are stacked to create a convenient place for storing and organizing photographs and correspondence.

Photo courtesy of Vitra, Inc.

With pegboard, *shelves can be adjusted to any height and spacing without damaging the wall surface. Though pegboard may be an unconventional wallcovering, it has practical advantages.*

(opposite, top) ***A desktop organizer*** *can eliminate cluttered desk syndrome. This unit features eight open shelves sized to hold mail, magazines and paperwork. Four drawers hold pens, staplers and other office necessities.*

(opposite, left) ***A dressing screen*** *can be used in a variety of ways. This one serves as a portfolio display. Dressing screens can also be used as room dividers to delineate your office area within a larger room.*

(opposite, bottom) ***A printer stand*** *with multiple shelves can store paper, ink cartridges, computer manuals and other items.*

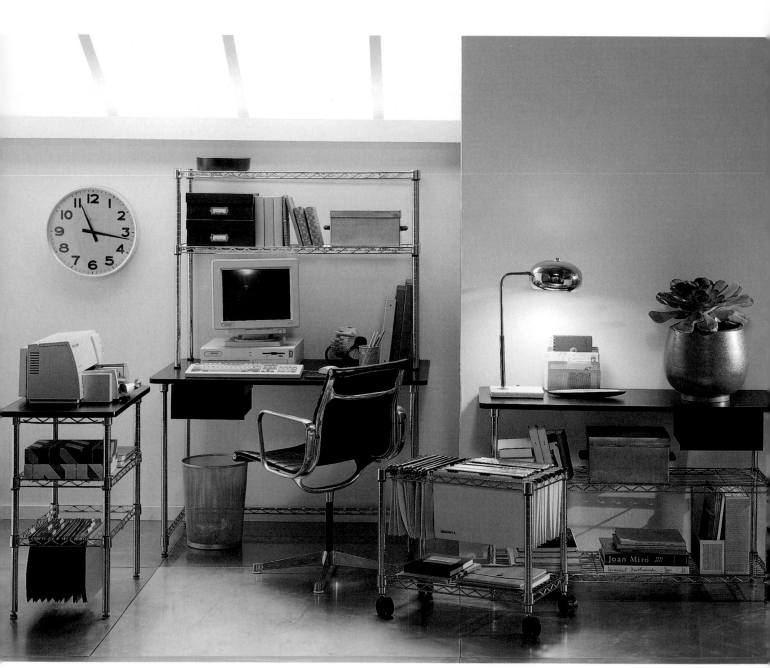

(above) ***Simple, coordinating furniture*** *gives this office an uncluttered, efficient ambience. The rolling file cart keeps paperwork accessible and organized.*

(left) *A computer hutch* efficiently stores computer equipment, which fits awkwardly on many conventional desks. Computers are available in either low-profile designs, which sit horizontally, or in tower configurations, which stand vertically. Here, the low-profile CPU sits on the shelf underneath the keyboard. On a conventional desk, a low-profile CPU often is placed directly under the monitor.

(below) *An extra-large* worksurface is helpful if you use a computer. The CPU and monitor can occupy a large area, so a wraparound desk, like the one shown here, can provide much-needed space. In this office, a large slide-out shelf holds the keyboard and mouse pad, freeing up additional desktop surface.

Essentials
COMPUTERS

Today, a desktop computer is nearly as essential to the home office as a desk and chair. Choosing the right computer can be a tough decision, since computers come in many different configurations and new features appear constantly. It is possible, however, to outline some of the basic choices you'll have when you set out to go computer shopping.

Operating system. Computers are classified as PCs or Macintosh, depending upon the operating system they use. Most PCs (personal computers) have Windows software as their operating system, while Macintosh computers have their own operating system. The critical factor in choosing between a PC or a Mac is the software you use, since some applications are designed to run on only one type of operating system. Note: most computers are sold with several software applications already installed, or bundled, as a standard sales feature.

CPU. Power, speed and hard-drive size are the main features to look for in CPUs (central processing units), and these are based on the type of processing chip and its operating speed (for example, Pentiums) as well as the speed, measured in megahertz. CPUs are getting faster all the time, so it's best to compare what's available and take advantage of this constantly evolving market. CPUs are fairly large (approximately 2'x 3'), so you may want to consider buying a "tower" unit that can be set on the floor vertically instead of sitting on the desktop. Tower units offer more expandability.

Disk and CD-ROM drive. Currently, most new computers include both internal 3.5" disk drives or ZIP drives, and internal CD-ROM drives. You may also want to consider buying an external storage device to use for backups.

Photo courtesy of Levenger

Desktop vs. laptop. If mobility is important to you, then a laptop, or notebook, computer may be the best choice for you. But there are tradeoffs involved; laptops have a smaller keyboard, and you'll pay more for a laptop than a desktop model with similar features and power. Laptops can also be uncomfortable to work at for long periods of time, but a docking station can alleviate this problem. Docking stations allow you to plug in your laptop to a larger screen and an expanded keyboard, providing the advantages of a desktop computer.

Modem. Modems connect your computer to the phone lines and are essential if you want to send E-mail or faxes or connect to the Internet. If you don't "surf the Web" now, you probably will in the future. Look for a computer with an internal modem built in. The higher the "baud rate," the faster the modem: a 56.6 modem is faster than a 33.6. If you already have a computer that doesn't have a modem, it's possible to add either an internal modem or an external modem that plugs in to the CPU.

Photo courtesy of Levenger

Photo courtesy of Room & Board

(top) ***A bed desk is perfect*** *for those who enjoy working in bed. A laptop computer fits neatly on top, and the two basket pedestals can be used to store magazines, legal pads or a cordless phone. (above)* ***Because of its size, a laptop computer*** *can be used on any desk. When you are finished with the computer, it can be folded up and put away—leaving you with an uncluttered desk.*

Monitor. Though a monitor is sometimes included as part of a package deal, you may choose to pay a little extra to upgrade to a monitor with a sharper screen and better color. You may also want to consider getting a larger screen (the minimum standard size is 15 inches) if you work with graphic-intensive applications. Other features to check are emission rates (there are low-emission models available) and the resolution, measured in dots per inch.

Keyboard. Typing at a computer keyboard can cause strain to your hands and arms, and manufacturers are constantly introducing new "ergonomic" styles, such as the Dvorak keyboard, that are designed to reduce this stress. Split keyboards and keyboards with different configurations are a few examples; try them out to see what works best for you.

Mouse. Like keyboards, computer mice are constantly being redesigned in the hopes of creating one that is easier on the hands and arms. Options to explore are track balls, stationary touch pads or styluses.

Memory and expansion. If you can't afford all the features you want now, look for a computer that you can upgrade at a later date—the minimum amount of memory these days is 32MBs. Being able to add more memory or other devices should extend the life of your computer for at least a few years.

Printer. The type of printer you choose—ink-jet, laser or dot-matrix—should be based primarily on what you can afford. Laser printers offer the highest quality, but they also cost the most; ink-jet printers have gotten better and better and are now very affordable. Dot-matrix printers are the least expensive, but they only make sense if you need to print on multilayer forms.

(top) **Ergonomic keyboards** *have an angled design so hands receive minimal stress. Such a keyboard, along with proper finger exercises, can greatly reduce the chances of injury from typing.*

(above) **Since the keyboard and mouse** *are the most frequently used components of a computer, it is important that they be at a comfortable height and position.*

(right) **The desktop computer's monitor** *and low-profile CPU sit on one shelf in this hutch desk. The keyboard is on a pull-out shelf, and the printer rests on a lower shelf. A large drop-down table provides a convenient worksurface.*

45

One of the most recent innovations is a combination printer/scanner/fax/copy machine; this may or may not be a good choice, depending on how much you plan to use each feature and on the quality level you need.

Personal organizer. Though digital datebooks and organizers have been around for quite a while, they've recently undergone some interesting changes. Organizers like the Palm Pilot, by 3Com, are small, hold large quantities of data and can be connected directly to computers for exchange of information.

A few final points to remember. It's important to arrange your keyboard and monitor at the right height and position to avoid physical strain to your hands and eyes (see Ergonomics, pg. 18). There are many desks, cabinets and workstations available that are designed specifically to hold computers, with adjustable shelves for keyboards and other components.

Regardless of the setup you choose, it's essential to have an adequate electrical supply for all of your equipment. You'll need at least one 20-amp circuit for your computer, another one if you have a copier that draws a lot of power. And you may want to consider adding a second phone line for your modem so you can send faxes and E-mail or connect to the Web without interrupting your voice phone service.

Use a surge protector to protect your equipment from damage that could occur when the power goes off and on suddenly (during a thunderstorm, for example). Also, look for wiring organizers that let you bunch wires together and get them out of sight.

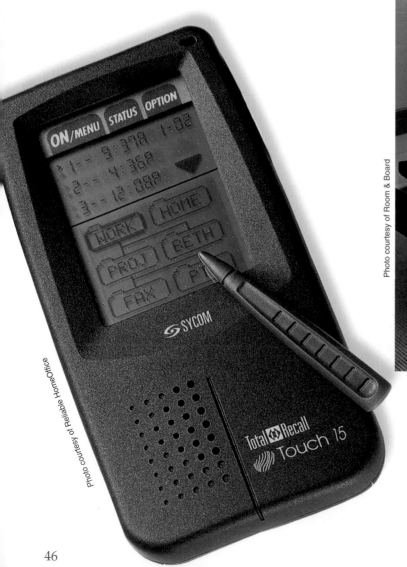

Photo courtesy of Reliable HomeOffice

Photo courtesy of Room & Board

(above) *A wiring organizer* bundles together the power cords and cables, eliminating tangles and protecting the cords.

(left) *Personal organizers* can be carried in a jacket pocket, attaché or even a purse. They can hold vast quantities of information that can be downloaded directly to computers. Some models feature a light pen and can recognize script, enabling the user to take notes as on a piece of paper.

(left) **A monitor and printer** can be placed on desktop organizers to conserve space. Just make sure the monitor is at the right viewing height.

(below) **A tower CPU offers** more expandability and is consequently more expensive. It can be stored either on the desk, or, more commonly, underneath the desk, where it is completely out of the way.

Essentials
COMMUNICATIONS

Communication is vital when you work out of your home, and modern technology has made it easier than ever to stay connected. Telephone service has expanded to include all kinds of useful features, and there are plenty of other tools available. A boon to telecommuters and home-based business owners, these devices help make the modern lifestyle possible.

Telephone. Features like call-waiting, voicemail and conference calling can greatly enhance your ability to reach people and, more important, remain accessible even if you only have one phone line. Adding a second phone line is a good idea if you send a lot of faxes and E-mail, or do work that requires being connected to the Internet. Cordless phones, speaker phones and telephone headsets can also be very convenient and help reduce neck strain. A 900 MHz cordless phone offers improved reception and security over a standard cordless phone.

Fax/modem machines. The fastest way to send copies of physical, rather than digitally stored, documents is using a fax/modem machine. There are two basic types of fax machines: plain-paper and thermal-paper models. Plain-paper fax machines cost much more than thermal-paper machines but they are generally a better choice, for several reasons. Thermal paper has a flimsy, waxy feel, and it turns dark when exposed to heat or light. More important, documents printed on thermal paper will fade over time. Most fax machines have memory that allows them to hold documents temporarily while they are waiting to be sent, as well as generate reports of faxes sent and received.

If you rarely have need to send physical documents but want to send a document from your computer screen to someone who has a fax machine, you can skip buying the fax machine and instead buy fax software to use with your computer's internal modem.

E-mail. Sending E-mail is easy and instantaneous. All you need is a computer with a modem, access to an on-line connection, and software to organize and prepare your correspondence for transmittal.

Cell phones and pagers. Being able to make or receive calls when you're on the move can make a huge difference when doing business, and cell phones and pagers are becoming more and more commonplace. Plus, the technology has evolved to the point that many standard phone features are now available with these portable devices.

(opposite) **Multiple phone lines** *are crucial for any business that relies heavily on phone connections to clients. In a fast-paced world, clients sometimes hate to wait.*

(right) **Cellular telephones** *have become a necessity for many people. Making a call while away from the office can save you time, money and business. The new technology offered by digital cell phones provides clearer reception and more secure communication than the old analog style.*

Choosing a variety of styles and materials for desk accessories helps create interest and texture.

Essentials

EXTRAS

In addition to the truly indispensible equipment and furniture every office needs, a few amenities can be just as essential—to your mental well-being. Just a few simple additions, like a stereo, coffee pot or microwave, can make your day much more enjoyable and productive. One of the primary advantages of working in a home office is that you can set up your workspace however you want, so there's no reason to limit yourself to a conventional office arrangement.

Aside from any "comfort" items, you may want to consider purchasing a few other practical items to make your work easier.

If you can afford it, for example, having your own copy machine can be a great convenience and can save you money over the long run. Office-supply catalogs are filled with all kinds of gadgets that can make work more interesting and efficient.

Personal items are also essential to a pleasant and productive home office. Family photos, artwork, plants and carefully chosen decorative accents can go a long way toward making your home office a place that is uniquely yours.

(above, top) **A bookend** *that doubles as a storage unit can help conserve needed space and make finding things just a bit easier.*

(right) **Streamlined and stylish,** *this stainless steel desk set provides an impressive solution for staying organized.*

EXTRAS

(right) **A water cooler** *in your office provides a healthy refreshment whenever you need it. Units such as these come with a handsome stand and an electric chiller.*

(below) **An editor's desk** *holds books and papers at an angle that is conducive to reading and taking notes. Since you don't have to hunch over a flat desk, the inclined position reduces fatigue and thereby increases productivity.*

(opposite top) **Office gadgets** *can add much-needed humor to a place of business. The gadgets shown here are functional accessories designed to resemble pieces of classic office equipment.*

(opposite bottom) **Desk accessories** *can make the task of organizing your office much easier. There are organizers for storing loose papers, letters, pencils, magazines, paper clips and self-adhesive note pads.*

Photos on this page courtesy of Reliable HomeOffice

A PORTFOLIO OF

HOME
OFFICE
IDEAS

DESIGNATED OFFICE SPACE

The advantages of a designated space for your home office are apparent.

By allocating a room for your home office needs, you nearly guarantee that your work will remain in one place, which has two benefits. First, papers and materials should be easier to find. And psychologically, it will be easier to focus on your work or remove yourself from it as needed.

A separate space also offers more privacy. If the kids have friends over, or you want to have a formal discussion with a client, you can close the door.

Creating a space for your home office can make planning easier, as well. If your office is a private space separate from the rest of the house, you can concern yourself with efficiency rather than style issues.

This office set in a bright, well-lit room has a large table spacious enough for two or three workers, or for meeting with clients. Space is also available for a desktop computer and shelving.

Photo courtesy of Vitra, Inc.

(above) **Built-in cabinets**, shelves and file drawers are the main features of this office. With the built-ins, all office materials can be kept in one area. Built-ins can be expensive, but the results are usually worth the investment.

(right) **A formal office** for receiving clients requires little more than a desk, a sitting chair and end table. Such an office can fit into a relatively small spare bedroom.

(opposite) **A designated space** for a home office allows you to decorate in almost any fashion. This office was designed with carved hardwood furniture and bookcases. French doors reduce sound but allow the handsome appearance of the office to be seen.

Space is not a limiting factor when you have a large spare room to dedicate as your home office. In these circumstances, you'll have room for a spacious desk, ample shelving and your choice of furniture and lighting fixtures.

61

Open shelving and low-profile *furniture create an airy, roomy environment in an office that is both attractive and efficient. A room with plentiful natural light is an ideal location for a home office that sees lots of use.*

Even a small space *can be dedicated to a home office, provided you make shrewd choices when selecting furniture and other features. In this office, the table can be fitted with extensions when work demands it. The movable computer cart takes up little space, but can still hold a printer, monitor and other accessories.*

LIVING ROOM OFFICE

There are several different ways you can go about setting up a home office in a living room, and each can work equally well. If your living room is large enough, you may want to create a separate "room" within the room by arranging your desk, chair and any equipment you use in one defined area. Another option is to purchase a piece of furniture that blends in with the decor but is designed for office use; for example, an armoire that contains a drop-down desk and room for a computer. This type of self-contained arrangement has the benefit of allowing you to hide your work away when it's time for relaxation or entertaining.

An armoire cabinet *can contain everything necessary for a home office, in a style that complements the decor of a room. When the armoire is closed the room is completely uncluttered and ready to be used for entertaining.*

Photo courtesy of Roche-Bobois

(above) **Floor-to-ceiling shelving** *is a good feature for a living room office. Here, accent lighting makes the unit attractive as well as practical.*

(right) **The corner of a living room** *can serve as an effective home office. The sleek, minimalist look of the furnishings make this home office unobtrusive.*

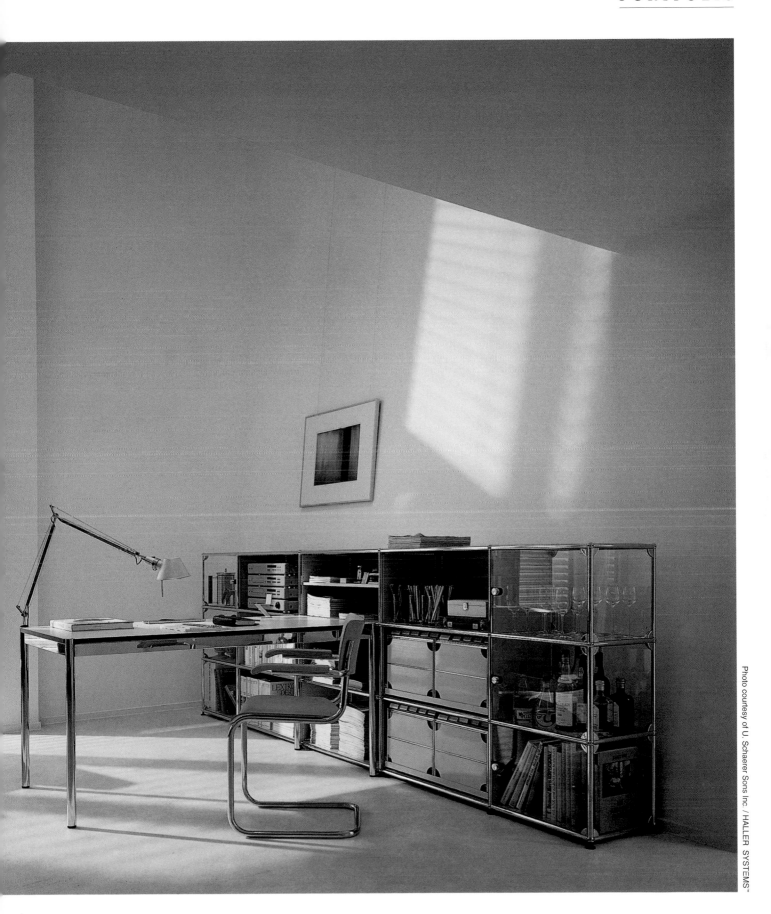

(right, below) **In these small homes,** each inhabited by a single dweller, the living room manages to hold not only a self-contained office, but an entertainment center and complete array of standard living room furniture. Organized storage is the key to making such an arrangement work.

(above) **Office furniture** chosen to match the painted trim moldings and natural wood flooring helps this corner office blend in nicely to the living room.

(right) **A corner desk and shelving unit** is a great way to make efficient use of space in a living room office. A computer and monitor occupy corner space that normally is wasted.

Photo courtesy of Exposures Catalog

(above) **An elegant desk and chair** transform this hallway into a convenient office. Using ordinary items, such as this umbrella stand, in a new way adds interest and function to your office space.

(left) **For some people,** design aesthetics take a priority over function in home office design. Richly upholstered chairs, an antiqued table and walls, and dark tones lend a European flair to this office.

73

KITCHEN OFFICE

The kitchen can be the ideal spot to set up a small office area to be used for bill paying, correspondence and other household management tasks. If you have enough space, you could set up a small desk off to the side of the room or simply use the kitchen table as a desk and designate a cabinet and a drawer or two for storage. Because this has become such a popular location for a home office, many new kitchens are designed with built-in desks and drawers that coordinate with the cabinetry. However, because the kitchen is often the busiest room in the house, you may have some difficulty finding enough peace and quiet for frequent work there.

An office directly off the dining room table is available whenever inspiration hits—over a second glass of wine at dinner, for example. The expansive windows in this example provide the office with lots of natural light and a view of the evening sunset.

Photo courtesy of Vitra, Inc.

(right) **This desk's file drawer** *provides a dedicated space for storing and organizing important paperwork, such as warranties, maintenance records and bills.*

(below) **Consistent styling and materials** *allow this kitchen office to blend effortlessly with the rest of the room. The fabric on the chair, which matches the window treatment, is a subtle and effective touch.*

All photos courtesy of Yorktowne® Cabinets

The built-in shelving *above and adjacent to the desk in this kitchen office provides practical, unobtrusive spaces for storing papers and displaying decorative items. If you're planning to remodel your kitchen, have the cabinetmaker or woodworker create a built-in desk and shelving to match the new counters and cabinets. A desk that matches the look and materials used in the rest of the kitchen won't seem out of place.*

(left) **A small office with computer** can easily fit in most kitchens. Here, a glass-block wall provides natural light while maintaining privacy.

(above) **Kitchen offices** can easily lend themselves to entertaining clients. Amenities such as the cappuccino maker shown above are readily available.

IKEA

(right) **Personal touches**—in this case, a
live plant and a framed photograph—add
an informal charm to this kitchen desk.

(below) **The undercabinet lighting** over
this desk provides ample task lighting
without taking up space on the desktop.

Photo courtesy of American Woodmark

Photo courtesy of KraftMaid Cabinetry, Inc.

Photo courtesy of KraftMaid Cabinetry, Inc.

The kitchen is the nerve center in many modern homes, making it the logical location for an office devoted to family business. If you like to be at the center of things and close to family members, a kitchen office might be the best solution for you. This office has built-in slots to store bills, keep track of important papers and store recipe cards.

BEDROOM OFFICE

It's usually quite easy to set up a home office in a bedroom. Most likely, the room already has adequate lighting, heating or cooling, and the electrical and phone wiring is already in place. Any additional outlets you might need can probably be installed fairly easily.

A spare bedroom is the best choice for a home office, but if space is limited, you can incorporate an office into an occupied bedroom. Finding enough office storage space may be a problem if the room serves double duty, but there are many creative ways to overcome this difficulty. Floor-to-ceiling shelving and a hideway sofa-bed, for example, are good choices for a bedroom that also serves as an office.

Photo courtesy of IKEA

A spare bedroom is an ideal location for a home office. The futon shown here is multifunctional, serving as a couch when the room is used as an office and as a bed when the room is needed for visiting family or friends.

(above) **Schoolchildren benefit** from having a bedroom office. An office like this one gives kids a private place to themselves for studying, working on homework and surfing the Internet.

(opposite) **Shelving is an important feature** to consider when designing a bedroom office, especially for students. These shelving units are large enough to comfortably house computer equipment and books, and even provide extra storage for bulky sweaters and blankets.

Photo courtesy of Sauder Woodworking Co.

(above) **This classic child's bedroom set** *is durable and looks good. It can also be converted to a guest bedroom as the child grows up.*

(opposite) **White bookshelves, desk and entertainment center** *allow the sun to reflect off the light-colored walls and make this bedroom look larger.*

Contemporary-styled shelves and chairs allow this office to blend harmoniously with the bedroom's open architecture and modern furnishings. A wing table opens outward to provide a worksurface and collapses into the wall for storage.

PORTABLE OFFICE

A portable office is perhaps the most convenient home office possibility of all. If you don't have an abundance of extra space, or cannot commit to a permanent location, a portable office is the ideal solution. All you need is an open nook or corner, a chair and a single piece of furniture to house your essential office equipment.

Many manufacturers are designing specialized computer consoles, complete with shelves, slide-out keyboard trays and a desktop just large enough to accommodate a monitor and a mouse. Larger models provide more desktop space and locations for additional office equipment, such as printers and fax machines. Some models, resembling small cabinets, can even fold up and conceal the contents inside. Many models roll on casters that allow you to store the office conveniently out of the way and move it to whatever location you desire.

Photo courtesy of Anthro Corp.

(right) **This sleek desk with a tall shelf** *fits in a small space. On this desk, the printer is out of the way, and the keyboard sits on a pull-out stand located at the correct height for typing. A cup of coffee can be placed on the convenient extension, eliminating the possibility of spilling liquids on the computer. The plant softens the austere appearance of the desk and computer.*

(opposite) **Larger consoles,** *like the one shown here, feature wide, adequate working space, shelving for your CPU and fax machine and a slide-out keyboard tray. Although it looks solid and heavy, this portable office rolls easily on hidden wheels.*

(opposite) **The tambour door** on this attractive console cabinet folds back to reveal an efficient and complete computer workstation.

(right, below) **This convertible cabinet** has two distinct personalities. When not in use, the sleek styling and cutwork pattern on the door accent the room. When unfolded, the cabinet transforms into a large portable office with built-in shelving, drawers, computer work area and even an "in" box.

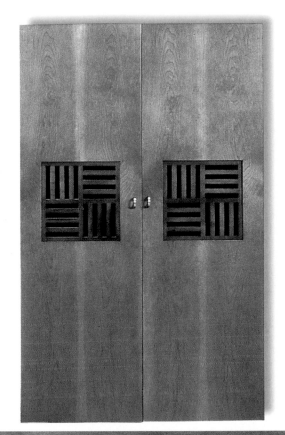

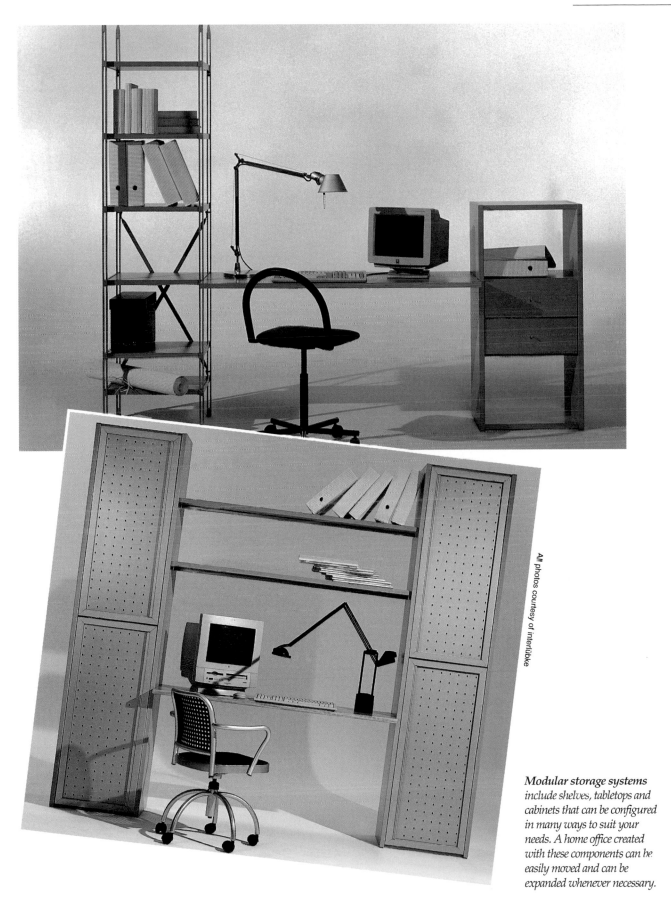

All photos courtesy of interlübke

Modular storage systems include shelves, tabletops and cabinets that can be configured in many ways to suit your needs. A home office created with these components can be easily moved and can be expanded whenever necessary.

LIST OF CONTRIBUTORS

We'd like to thank the following companies for providing the photographs used in this book:

American Woodmark
3102 Shawnee Drive, PO Box 1980
Winchester, VA 22601
(800) 292-2935

Andersen Windows, Inc.
100 Fourth Avenue North
Bayport, MN 55003-1096
(612) 439-5150

Anthro Corp.
10450 S.W. Manhasset Drive
Tualatin, OR 97062
(800) 325-3841

Artemide Inc.
1980 New Highway
Farmingdale, NY 11735
(516) 694-9292

Broyhill Furniture Industries, Inc.
One Broyhill Park
Lenoir, NC 28633-0001
(704) 758-3111

Brueton
145-68 228th Street
Springfield Gardens, NY 11413
(800) 221-6783

Drexel Heritage Furnishings, Inc.
101 North Main Street
Drexel, NC 28619
(800) 916-1986

Dura Supreme, Inc.
300 Dura Drive, PO Box K
Howard Lake, MN 55349
(320) 543-3872

Ergonomic Logic, Inc.
205 Vista Boulevard, #101
Sparks, NV 89434
(800) 433-6614

Exposures Catalog
27 Ann Street
South Norwalk, CT 06854
(203) 854-1610

Herman Miller for the Home
855 East Main Street
Zeeland, MI 49464
(800) 646-4400

Hold Everything
PO Box 7807
San Francisco, CA 94120-7807
(800) 421-2264

IKEA
496 West Germantown Pike
Plymouth Meeting, PA 19462
East Coast: (410) 931-8940
West Coast: (818) 912-1119

interlübke
PO Box 139
Athens, NY 12015
(518) 945-1007

Kinesis Corporation
22121 17th Avenue S.E., Suite 112
Bothell, WA 98021-7404
(425) 402-8100

Knoll, Inc.
1235 Water Street
East Greenville, PA 18041
(800) 445-5045

KraftMaid Cabinetry, Inc.
15535 S. State Avenue, PO Box 1055
Middlefield, OH 44062
(800) 571-1990

Levenger
420 South Congress Avenue
Delray Beach, FL 33445-4696
(800) 544-0880

Merillat Industries, Inc.
PO Box 1946
Adrian, MI 49221
(517) 263-0771

Motorola - Cellular Subscriber Sector
600 North U.S. Highway 45
Libertyville, IL 60048
(847) 523-5000

Reliable HomeOffice
PO Box 1501
Ottawa, IL 61350
(800) 869-6000

Roche-Bobois
183 Madison Avenue
New York, NY 10016
(800) 972-8375

Room & Board
4600 Olson Memorial Highway
Minneapolis, MN 55422
(800) 486-6554

Sanus Systems
619 West County Road E
St. Paul, MN 55126
(612) 484-7988

Sauder Woodworking Co.
502 Middle Street
Archbold, OH 43502
(800) 537-8560

Smith Metal Arts/
Smith McDonald Corp.
304 Senwil Drive
Buffalo, NY 14225
(800) 753-8548

Techline Furniture
500 S. Division St.
Waunakee, WI 53597
(800) 356-8400

Turnstone/Steelcase Inc.
PO Box 2608
Grand Rapids, MI 49501
(616) 698-5857

U. Schaerer Sons Inc./
HALLER SYSTEMS™
150 East 58th Street
New York, NY 10155
(212) 371-1230

Vitra, Inc.
149 Fifth Avenue
New York, NY 10010
(800) 33-VITRA

Wellington Hall LTD
PO Box 1354
Lexington, NC 27293-1354
(336) 249-4931

Yorktowne® Cabinets
100 Redco Avenue
Red Lion, PA 17356
(717) 244-4011